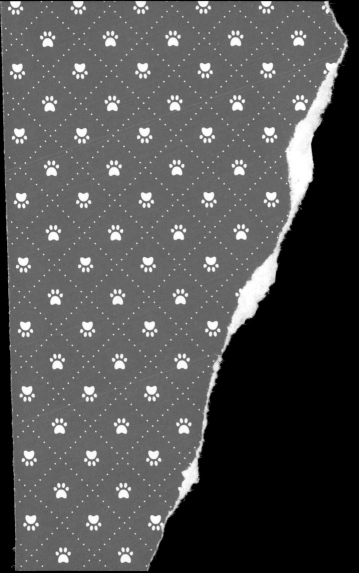

A gift for

_____

From

_____

Date

_____

insbearations

Warm and Wise Words of Encouragement

Ron Winnegrad

ℬℬ

Bright & Happy Books

Montclair, NJ

BB

Published by Bright & Happy Books, LLC
Montclair, NJ 07042

insBEARations

LC Control Number: 2016961780
ISBN 978-1-946477-00-2

The author and the publisher have made every effort to ensure that the quotes compiled in this book are properly attributed.

The Seven Steps of Happiness reprinted with the kind permission of Doe Zantamata. You can find more of her work at happinessinyourlife.com.

Printed in Malaysia by Tien Wah Press.

1 3 5 7 9 11 13 15 17 19 20 18 16 14 12 10 8 6 4 2

Introduction

I have a teddy bear by the name of Grizz. Thirty-seven years ago, one of my customers gave him to me. I was single at the time, and she thought I could use a friend. He was my very first teddy bear—I'd never had one as a child. After giving him a name, I felt bad leaving him at home all day, so I brought him to work. I felt even worse leaving him alone in the office at night, so I started carrying him back and forth to work with me in his own special sack.

Everybody in the perfume industry got to know Grizz. He was by my side when I met with colleagues; I brought him with me when I made presentations to customers. They always looked forward to seeing him. Grizz brought a smile to everyone who met him.

After a few years, the company I worked for merged with another one, and my new boss forbade me from taking Grizz on customer visits. I said, "Okay." When my boss and I went to our first appointment together after that, the customer immediately asked, "Where's Grizz?" I told her about the new rules, and she looked right at my boss and said, "If Grizz is not at the next meeting, don't bother coming back." Grizz was back at the table for all future visits with our customers.

Sure, we could have done those presentations without him, but having Grizz there made the meetings more fun. Happiness, it seems, is not about having everything you want, but about finding meaning, connection, and fulfillment in all the things you do.

I wanted to find a small way to repay the loyalty and kindness of this customer and everyone in my life who had supported me. That year, I painted a Christmas card of Grizz and gave copies to friends, customers, and colleagues. I received lots of warm responses. The next year, I made cards for Valentine's Day, Easter, and Halloween, too. I soon found I could give even more happiness to these people by sending out a card every month.

That's how the insBEARation cards came about. They inspired people and helped them through some difficult and stressful times. And now I hope this book of insBEARations will put a smile on *your* face and hope in your heart, too. With a few wise, warm words of encouragement, we can all do big things.

Grizz and I thank you.

Ron Winnegrad

insbearations

The most important questions in life
can never be answered by anyone
except oneself.

— John Fowles

The Magus

The reward for conformity is that
everyone likes you except yourself.

— Rita Mae Brown

Staying vulnerable is a risk we have to take if we want to experience connection.

— Brené Brown
The Gifts of Imperfection

You must love in such a way that the

person you love feels free.

— Thích Nhất Hạnh

Everything in the universe has a rhythm, everything dances.

— Maya Angelou

To be aware of a single shortcoming within oneself is more useful than to be aware of a thousand in somebody else.

— His Holiness the Dalai Lama

The Path to Enlightenment

Yesterday I was clever, so I wanted to change the world. Today I am wise, so I am changing myself.

— Anonymous

Confidence is belief in yourself. Certainty is belief in your beliefs. Confidence is a bridge. Certainty is a barricade.

— Kevin Ashton

How to Fly a Horse

Those with knowledge seek certainty,

but the one who is certain

yearns for insight.

— *Rumi*
Day by Day

If your ego prevents you from evolving, remove its "E."

— Catherine Lepage
Thin Slices of Anxiety

Be yourself. Everyone else is already taken.

— Anonymous

The usefulness of a cup is

in its emptiness. . . .

If you want to become full,

let yourself be empty.

— Laozi

Tao Te Ching

Change is the law of life.

And those who look only to the

past or the present are certain

to miss the future.

— John F. Kennedy

One has to decide whether one's
fears or one's hopes are what
should matter most.

— Atul Gawande

Being Mortal

He who conquers others is strong; he
who conquers himself is mighty.

— *Laozi*
Tao Te Ching

Of all the virtues we can learn, no trait is more useful, more essential for survival, and more likely to improve the quality of life than the ability to transform adversity into an enjoyable challenge.

— Mihály Csíkszentmihályi
Flow: The Psychology of Optimal Experience

Only those who will risk going

too far can possibly find out how

far one can go.

— *T.S. Eliot*

preface to *Transit of Venus* by Harry Crosby

It's only those who do nothing

that make no mistakes.

— *Joseph Conrad*
An Outcast of the Islands

Ten years from now, make sure you
can say that you chose your life,
you didn't settle for it.

— *Mandy Hale*
The Single Woman

Plan in decades. Think in years.

Work in months. Live in days.

— Nic Haralambous

Only he who attempts the absurd is capable of achieving the impossible.

— Miguel de Unamuno

If we did all the things we are capable of doing, we would literally astound ourselves.

— Thomas Edison

I've failed over and over and over again in my life. And that is why I succeed.

— Michael Jordan

Never mistake activity

for achievement.

— John Wooden

Your assumptions are your windows
on the world. Scrub them off every
once in a while, or the light
won't come in.

— Alan Alda

Develop your own compass, and trust it. Take risks, dare to fail, remember the first person through the wall always gets hurt.

—Aaron Sorkin

Nothing is more exhausting than the task that is never started.

— Gretchen Rubin

Better Than Before

Even a happy life cannot be without
a measure of darkness, and the word
"happy" would lose its meaning if it
were not balanced by sadness.

— Carl Jung
The Art of Living

Avoidance is a wonderful therapy.

— Maggie Stiefvater

Linger

Attention is the rarest and purest form of generosity.

— Simone Weil
Gravity and Grace

Walk away from "friendships" that make you feel small and insecure, and seek out people who inspire you and support you.

— Michelle Obama

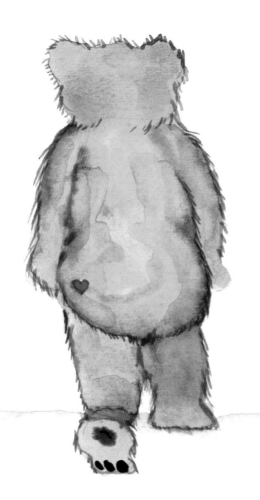

Mistakes are always forgivable, if one

has the courage to admit them.

— Bruce Lee

Everything will change when your desire to move on exceeds your desire to hold on.

— Alan H. Cohen

With an open mind and a forgiving heart, I see every person as superior to me in some way; with every person as my teacher, I grow in wisdom. As I grow in wisdom, humility becomes ever more my guide.

— Eric Greitens

Resilience

A humble person rarely stumbles, the old ones say, because such a person walks with face toward the Earth and can see the path ahead. On the other hand, the arrogant man who walks with his head high to bask in the glory of the moment will stumble often because he is more concerned with the moment than what lays ahead.

— Joseph M. Marshall III
The Lakota Way

The Creator gave you two ears and one mouth, so you can listen twice as much as you speak.

— Onondaga proverb

Embrace the eight pillars of joy.

— His Holiness the Dalai Lama
and Archbishop Desmond Tutu

The Book of Joy

Think less, feel more. Frown less, smile more. Talk less, listen more. Judge less, accept more. Watch less, do more. Complain less, appreciate more. Fear less, love more.

— *Doe Zantamata*
One Page Stories, Volume One

The happiest people don't have the best of everything; they just make the best of everything.

— Anonymous

Growing older is certain; growing wiser is harder and optional.

— Debasish Mridha

The purpose of life is to discover your gift. The work of life is to develop it. The meaning of life is to give your gift away.

— David Viscott
Finding Your Strength in Difficult Times

You are imperfect, permanently and inevitably flawed. And you are beautiful.

— *Amy Bloom*

"Dear Every Woman I Know, Including Me"

When in doubt, be ridiculous.

— Sherwood Smith

Beauty

Don't cry because it's over!

Smile because it happened!

— Ludwig Jacobowski

"Bright Days"